TAKE CHARGE!

▲▲▲▲▲▲▲▲▲▲

BOOK 1

TAKE CHARGE!

A Student-Centered Approach to English

Edna T. Diolata

The McGraw-Hill Companies, Inc.
New York St. Louis San Francisco Auckland Bogotá Caracas
Lisbon London Madrid Mexico City Milan Montreal
New Delhi San Juan Singapore Sydney Tokyo Toronto

To Chad

▼ ▼ ▼ ▼ ▼ ▼ ▼ ▼ ▼ ▼ ▼ ▼ ▼ ▼ ▼

McGraw-Hill

A Division of The McGraw-Hill Companies

Take Charge!
A Student-Centered Approach to English
Book One

1 2 3 4 5 6 7 8 9 0 QPD QPD 9 0 0 9 8 7

ISBN 0-07-044427-7

This book was set in Century Schoolbook by The Clarinda Company. The editors were Tim Stookesberry and John Chapman; the text and cover designer was Vargas/Williams design; the production supervisor was Michelle Lyon; illustrations were done by David Bohn, Robin Dewitt, Edna Diolata, Eldon Doty, Function Thru Form, Inc., Anica Gibson, Rick Hackney, Karel Hayes, Stephanie O'Shaughnessy, Charlie Shaw, George Ulrich, Randy Veroughstraete; interior icons were designed by Marcus Badgley; project management was done by J. Carey Publishing Service.

Quebecor Press Dubuque, Inc. was printer and binder. Phoenix Color Corporation was cover separator and printer.

Library of Congress Catalog Card Number: 96-79543

http://www.mhcollege.com

Contents

▼▼▼▼▼▼▼▼▼▼▼▼

To the Teacher

▼ ▼ ▼ ▼ ▼ ▼ ▼ ▼ ▼ ▼ ▼ ▼ ▼

Take Charge! is a two-level series for adult ESOL students featuring:

▼ a student-centered approach;

▼ a focus on useful language;

▼ opportunities for authentic communication;

▼ early literacy training;

▼ practice in critical thinking skills;

▼ an optional grammar component.

Perhaps the most unique aspect of *Take Charge!* is its focus on student-centered teaching, which helps students empower themselves in language learning and, ultimately, in everyday life. In the words of Brazilian educator Paulo Freire: "Adult education should have as one of its main tasks to invite people to believe in themselves. It should invite people to believe that they have knowledge." This series does not adhere to a single approach or methodology. Instead, it integrates a number of methodologies, emphasizing those that maximize student interaction and involvement.

The strong content strand in *Take Charge!* features language that will help students function effectively in both work and inter-personal situations. In addition, the materials provide early literacy training, allow for a balance of the four language skills, and promote critical thinking skills.

Take Charge! is designed to actively involve students in the language-learning process. Adult learners bring with them a rich variety of cultural and linguistic backgrounds. This series helps teachers make the most of these resources—providing personal motivation for each individual and a more exciting and effective learning environment for everyone.

Recommended Proficiency Levels

Level One of the *Take Charge!* program is for students who have had little exposure to English and may not be fully literate in a first language. Each lesson begins with a visual introduction to the theme, followed by key vocabulary items. Students then move from controlled listening and speaking exercises to more open-ended activities in all four skill areas. Each lesson concludes with a student story, paired activities, and a general review.

Level Two of the *Take Charge!* program is intended for more advanced beginners who already know some English and have acquired some fundamental literacy skills. Each lesson contains about 20 individual activities that provide a starting point for introducing and developing language related to the unit theme.

	BEST Scores	CASAS Achievement Scores	MELT SPLs
Take Charge! Level One	0–25	165–195	0 and I
Take Charge! Level Two	26–50	185–210	II and III

The *Take Charge!* series is compatible with the Comprehensive Adult Student Assessment System (CASAS) and the Student Performance Levels (SPLs) disseminated by the Mainstream English Language Training (MELT) project. The SPL scores shown above are correlated with scores on the Basic English Skills Test (BEST). In addition, the two books in the *Take Charge!* program conform to the California Model Standards. Level One is appropriate for Beginning-Low programs, and Level Two fits Beginning-High programs.

A Complete Learning Package

Both levels of the *Take Charge!* program feature the following components:

Student Text

At each level, the **Student Text** features the basic language students need to function in a variety of contexts in the English-speaking community. The **Student Text** contains meaningful learning tasks and provides many opportunities for students to communicate with one another in English. Each unit includes a balance of practice in the four language skills. Throughout the series, students are invited to engage in critical thinking and reflection about personal experiences as well as current social issues.

Grammar Workbook

Both **Grammar Workbooks** in the *Take Charge!* series contain simple explanations of selected grammar items that appear in each **Student Text**, along with several practice exercises on each point. The **Grammar Workbook** can be used in class or as a self-study program with periodic teacher follow-up. A complete answer key is found at the end of each book.

Teacher's Edition

Both **Teacher's Editions** contain step-by-step suggestions for presenting all **Student Text** and **Grammar Workbook** lessons. Each lesson in the **Teacher's Edition** opens with a general explanation and overview of the material covered in that lesson, followed by detailed teaching suggestions.

Audio Program

At each level, the **Audio Program** contains vocabulary words for students to repeat, listening activities, practice dialogues, and other exercise material. If the teacher chooses to read this material to the class, the **Audio Program** can be used for individual or small-group review and practice. A complete tapescript for the **Audio Program** can be found at the back of the **Student Text**.

ACKNOWLEDGMENTS

Special thanks to my editor, John Chapman, for his guidance and support. I would also like to acknowledge the McGraw-Hill editorial and production team who helped bring these materials to fruition: Tim Stookesberry, Bill Preston, Brett Glass, Shannon McIntyre (of Function Thru Form, Inc.), Francis Owens, and Jennifer Carey (of J. Carey Publishing Service). Finally, I'd like to thank Thalia Dorwick, Andy Martin, and the rest of the McGraw-Hill sales and marketing department for their outstanding support.

I would also like to acknowledge the contributions of the following reviewers who made many useful suggestions that helped shape this book: Michelle Alvarez, Laura Berry, Jeffrey Bright, Lauri Fried-Lee, Elizabeth Granados, Ellen Harley, Marjorie Henderson, Emily Lites, Robin Longshaw, Pete LoPresti, Sue Nelson, Barbara A. Shaw, Csilla B. Shinkle, Marcia Taylor, and Marian Tyson.

Finally, special thanks go to my students, who are my teachers and who are the inspiration for this book.

Edna T. Diolata
Brooklyn, New York

Highlights of
▼▼▼▼▼▼▼▼▼▼▼▼▼▼
TAKE CHARGE! Book One

All units in **Take Charge!,** Student Book 1 are 12 pages long. Units have a consistent, predictable format which makes the material easy for students and teachers to use. The next few pages are designed to highlight the purpose of various features and activities, and provide teaching suggestions you might use with the material. More detailed explanations of teaching methods as well as complete chapter lessons are found in the **Teacher's Edition.**

Clear, Lively Illustrations

The first page in each unit features a large drawing (or a group of smaller drawings) that illustrates the theme of the unit and can be used for a variety of exercises and activities. *Note:* the drawings found on this page were all done by the author of the student text, Edna Diolata.

UNIT 3 **School**

Words
student pen book clock
teacher chair notebook eraser
paper table calendar dictionary

Point to the people and things
Say the words

Unit Opening Page

The opening page is designed to introduce students to the thematic content of the unit and activate their prior knowledge of this content. As they are invited to identify objects in the picture, ask questions, and share information, students build confidence, interest, and motivation.

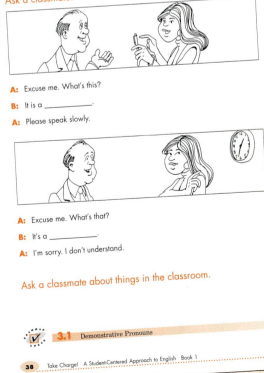

Ask a classmate.

A: Excuse me. What's this?
B: It is a _____.
A: Please speak slowly.

A: Excuse me. What's that?
B: It's a _____.
A: I'm sorry. I don't understand.

Ask a classmate about things in the classroom.

☑ **3.1** Demonstrative Pronouns

Abundant Vocabulary Practice

Key vocabulary is practiced in both the **Student Book** and the accompanying **Audio Program,** allowing students to both hear and see important new words that they are expected to master.

Numerous Opportunities for Pair Work

Many of the exercises and activities in **Take Charge!** allow students to interact with one another in partner situations. In the examples on this page, students practice in pairs first, and then complete a follow-up conversation activity.

Start Talking

The third and fourth pages of each unit feature activities designed to give students additional listening and speaking practice with the target language. These early exercises provide plenty of support as students begin to use the language in meaningful interactive situations.

Integrated Skills Activities

Many of the activities in this book take an integrated approach to teaching the four basic English skills: listening, speaking, reading, and writing. The exercises on page 39, for example, integrate reading, listening and speaking, and writing.

The material on page 40 leads students through a sequence involving listening and reading, listening and speaking, and writing.

Use of Visual Cues

Many speaking and writing activities are cued by pictures. These nonverbal cues provide visual contexts that help students to understand the language focus.

Start Talking

Ask a classmate.

A: Do you need paper?

B: Yes, I do.

A: Here you are.

B: Thank you very much.

A: What do you need?

B: I need a _____.

A: Here you are.

B: Thank you very much.

Write.

1. _____
2. _____
3. _____
4. _____
5. _____

Start Talking

Look and listen. Do the actions.

 Enter the room.

 Turn on the light.

 Turn off the light.

 Leave the room.

Ask the teacher to do the actions. Ask a classmate to do the actions. Write the actions.

1. _____

2. _____

3. _____

4. _____

x

Look Again

Write

Ff ___ ___ ___

Vv ___ ___ ___

🎵 Listen and repeat.

1. **f**our **v**erb
2. **f**rom **v**ery
3. **f**ifty se**v**en
4. wi**f**e lea**v**e
5. o**ff** ha**v**e

🎵 Listen and write **f** or **v**.

1. ___or
2. No___ember
3. ___i___teen
4. li___e
5. ___riday
6. twel___e
7. ___i___e
8. ___ebruary

🎵 Listen and write the word.

1. Where do you _____?
2. Are you _____ Africa?
3. Today is _____.
4. Thank you _____ much.

Unit 3   School   **41**

Look Again

The fifth and sixth pages of each unit are titled **Look Again**. The activities on these pages give students a closer look at the language and content introduced earlier. Here students refine pronunciation, practice listening and speaking skills, and begin to apply the material to their own lives.

Abundant Listening Practice

A cassette icon indicates that the activity is featured in the **Audio Program**. The exercises on this page provide an opportunity for students to listen to key pronunciation items as many times as they wish while completing the activities. In other parts of the unit, the **Audio Program** provides model dialogues and contextualized listening passages.

Students Bring Their Own Experiences to the Classroom

The goal of any student-centered approach is to personally involve each learner in the curriculum as many as possible. Each unit of *Take Charge!* contains many exercises and activities such as this one, where students are invited to discuss actual situations from their own lives.

Grammar Checks

All grammar in the *Take Charge!* program is contextualized within the themes found in the student text. The actual explanations and exercises for each grammar point are found in the accompanying **Grammar Workbook** for each level, allowing teachers the flexibility to highlight essential grammar content as they feel appropriate for their particular group of students.

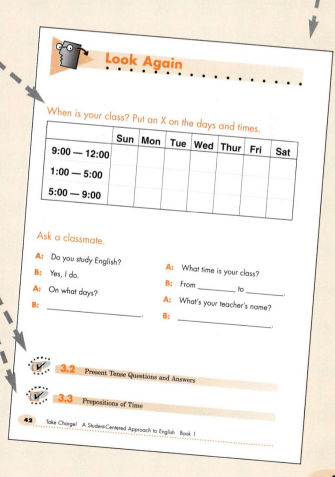

Look Again

When is your class? Put an X on the days and times.

	Sun	Mon	Tue	Wed	Thur	Fri	Sat
9:00 — 12:00							
1:00 — 5:00							
5:00 — 9:00							

Ask a classmate.

A: Do you study English?

B: Yes, I do.

A: On what days?

B: _____.

A: What time is your class?

B: From _____ to _____.

A: What's your teacher's name?

B: _____.

3.2 Present Tense Questions and Answers

3.3 Prepositions of Time

42 Take Charge! A Student-Centered Approach to English Book 1

Keep Talking

The seventh and eighth pages of each unit provide a variety of activities to help students develop confidence and fluency with the new language presented in the unit. These pages also introduce additional vocabulary words and language forms carefully tailored to the unit theme.

Dealing with Feelings

Each unit of *Take Charge!* deals with personal or emotional situations that students may be encountering in their own everyday lives. These activities help students learn to express their feelings in English, which is an important element in learning to cope with life in North America.

Variety of Exercise and Activity Types

One of the goals of the *Take Charge!* program is to keep students actively involved in the learning process. Therefore, students are exposed to a number of different types of exercises and activities to allow for maximum creativity in the classroom. This particular example is a variation of a standard pattern practice dialogue: students play "reporter" by interviewing their teacher and classmates, then recording the information they learn in a simple chart.

Reading

The ninth page always features a culminating reading based on the theme of the unit. Most of these readings deal with issues directly pertaining to students' lives. These readings progress in difficulty throughout the **Student Book 1**.

Illustrations accompany all readings, promoting student interest and greatly aiding comprehension. The reading passages themselves are carefully controlled to be of appropriate length and difficulty for beginning students.

Writing

Writing activities are kept simple throughout the book. Here students get several forms of input to support them as they begin writing in English. They listen to the story one or more times and get clues from the picture. The fill-in format allows them to write single words within the framework of a contextualized passage.

Look at the picture. Listen to the story.

APRIL

Tell the story. Write the story.

It is _____ morning. I _____ in class. The

_____ is _____. The _____ are

_____. One student is _____. Another student is

confused. We are all _____.

Unit 3   School   **45**

Writing tasks in these units progress from simple to complex. Students learn to print individual letters and numbers, copy words and phrases, write dictated words and phrases, fill in blanks with words, and, at the end, answer questions in complete sentences.

Two-Way Review

The tenth and eleventh pages of each unit feature an interactive review of all the material presented in the previous pages. Students are asked to work in pairs and quiz each other using the several sets of questions on each page. This review allows students to gauge their own progress and set goals for improvements as they proceed through the rest of the book.

TWO-WAY REVIEW

STUDENT A

Work with a partner. One of you works with this page. The other works with page 47. Don't look at your partner's page.

Ask your partner.

1. What's this?
2. What are you doing?
3. What time is your class?
4. What's your teacher's name?

Circle the answer.

1. It's an eraser.
   Thank you.

2. I'm fine.
   Yes, I need paper.

3. Yes, I do.
   Yes, I am.

4. From 6:00 to 8:00 P.M.
   From Monday to Friday.

Spell the words to your partner. Write the letters you hear.

1. T H U R S D A Y
2. A U G U S T
3. C A L E N D A R
4. S T U D E N T

1. _ _ _ _ _ _ _ _
2. _ _ _ _ _ _ _ _
3. _ _ _ _ _ _ _ _
4. _ _ _ _ _ _ _ _

46   Take Charge! A Student-Centered Approach to English Book 1

Two-Way Review

Notice that one student looks only at page 47 and the other looks only at page 46. The exercise material is designed so that students not only ask each other the questions, but also help each other formulate the answers when needed. This fosters a cooperative learning atmosphere and helps make the activity a learning experience instead of a testing situation.

General Review

The General Review is designed as an independent review and expansion of the language and concepts introduced in the unit. Depending on your individual situation, you may wish to assign it as homework, or ask students to complete it in pairs or small groups in class.

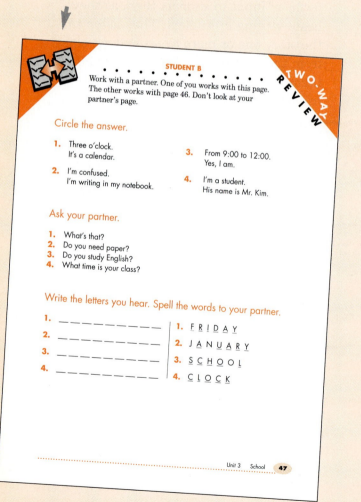

About the Author

▼ ▼ ▼ ▼ ▼ ▼ ▼ ▼ ▼ ▼ ▼ ▼ ▼ ▼

Edna T. Diolata has taught ESOL for 13 years, in New York City and at the Philippine Refugee Processing Center in Morong, Bataan, the Philippines. In New York, she has taught at the Consortium for Worker Education and at the CAMBA Even Start Program.

In addition to being an experienced English teacher, Edna is also an accomplished artist. She has provided the illustrations for all the chapter-opening pages in this book.

The Alphabet and Numbers

Words

print   read   circle   sign

A   B   C   D   E   F

→

G   H   I   J   K   L

M   N   O   P   Q   R

S   T   U   V   W   X

Y   Z

Draw arrows under the alphabet.
Say the words.

Circle the letter.

1. **A**	A	H	H	A	H
2. **B**	P	B	B	P	P
3. **E**	F	E	F	F	E
4. **F**	F	E	F	E	E
5. **G**	C	G	C	G	C
6. **J**	L	J	L	L	J
7. **K**	K	X	K	X	K
8. **M**	N	M	N	M	N
9. **N**	N	N	M	N	M
10. **P**	B	P	P	B	P
11. **Q**	G	Q	G	G	Q
12. **R**	B	B	R	B	R
13. **U**	U	V	U	V	V
14. **W**	M	W	W	M	M
15. **Y**	X	X	Y	X	Y
16. **Z**	S	Z	S	Z	S

 Listen and circle.

1. V   A   K   K   A   V

2. E   F   F   I   E   I

3. T   H   T   M   H   T

4. M   M   N   H   H   N

5. Q   Q   Q   O   O   Q

6. B   V   P   P   B   V

7. K   X   X   S   S   K

8. I   T   I   T   T   L

9. L   T   T   I   I   L

10. W   W   V   B   V   B

11. B   V   B   P   P   V

12. J   J   G   G   C   C

13. U   Y   Y   Q   U   Q

14. H   H   X   F   F   X

15. L   L   R   L   R   L

16. Y   I   I   Y   A   A

Write the letters.

A A   B B   C C   D D

E E   F F   G G   H H

I I   J J   K K   L L

M M   N N   O O   P P

Q Q   R R   S S   T T

U U   V V   W W   X X

Y Y   Z Z

Circle the letter.

1. **a**	a	c	c	a	c
2. **d**	d	b	b	b	d
3. **o**	o	a	a	o	o
4. **p**	b	p	p	b	b
5. **t**	t	f	f	t	t
6. **l**	i	l	i	l	i
7. **i**	i	l	i	l	l
8. **j**	j	i	j	j	i
9. **g**	g	p	g	p	g
10. **r**	n	r	n	n	r
11. **q**	g	q	g	q	q
12. **e**	e	s	s	e	s
13. **u**	v	u	v	u	v
14. **v**	v	w	v	w	w
15. **s**	s	e	s	e	s
16. **m**	n	n	n	m	m

 Listen and circle.

1. a	c	c	a	c
2. g	p	p	g	p
3. d	b	b	d	d
4. r	n	r	r	n
5. i	t	i	i	t
6. f	s	f	f	s
7. t	l	t	l	l
8. y	g	g	y	g
9. c	o	o	c	c
10. n	r	n	r	n
11. z	c	z	c	z
12. s	s	s	x	x
13. b	p	p	b	b
14. i	i	e	e	e
15. a	e	e	a	e
16. q	q	u	q	u

Write the letters.

a   b   c   d

_____   _____   _____   _____

e   f   g   h

_____   _____   _____   _____

i   j   k   l

_____   _____   _____   _____

m   n   o   p

_____   _____   _____   _____

q   r   s   t

_____   _____   _____   _____

u   v   w   x

_____   _____   _____   _____

y   z

_____   _____

Listen and repeat.

0   1   2   3   4   5   6   7   8   9   10

Write the numbers.

0 _____ _____ _____

1 _____ _____ _____

2 _____ _____ _____

3 _____ _____ _____

4 _____ _____ _____

5 _____ _____ _____

6 _____ _____ _____

7 _____ _____ _____

8 _____ _____ _____

9 _____ _____ _____

10 _____ _____ _____

Circle the number.

zero	one	zero	one	zero
one	one	two	two	one
two	ten	two	two	ten
three	ten	three	ten	ten
four	five	four	four	four
five	five	nine	nine	five
six	two	six	two	six
seven	three	three	seven	seven
eight	eight	eight	three	eight
nine	five	nine	five	nine
ten	two	ten	ten	two

Look and read.

Listen.

Circle.

Read.

Write.

Say.

Ask and answer.

Match.

Write.

Read.

Listen.

Circle.

Ask and answer.

Say.

 Listen and write.

Letters	**Numbers**
1. __ __ __ __	1. __ __
2. __ __ __	2. __ __
3. __ __ __	3. __ __
4. __ __ __ __ __	4. __ __
5. __ __ __ __ __ __	5. __ __

Introductions

Words

Hello   name   first   last   my   your

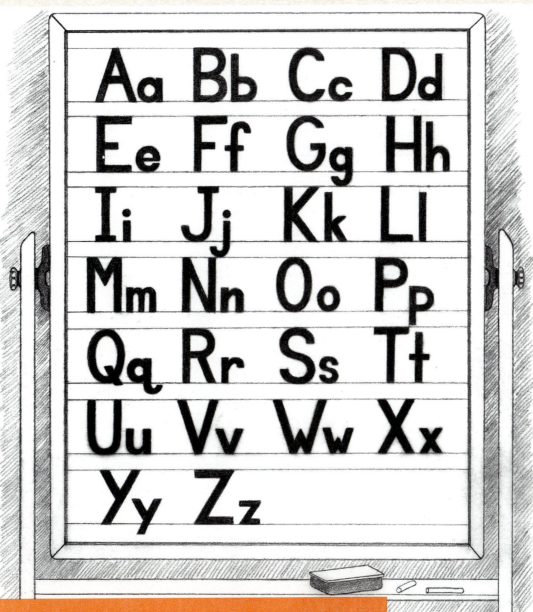

Say the alphabet.
Say the words.

Circle the different letter.

 Listen and circle the letter.

	Circle the different letter	Listen and circle the letter
1.	F F F F (E) F	E F L (T)
2.	T T I T T T	D B P R
3.	O O O O O C	O Q C G
4.	r r r n r r	c a d b
5.	g g g g g q	g q p b

Write the alphabet.

_____	Bb	_____	_____	Ee
Ff	_____	Hh	_____	_____
Kk	_____	Mm	_____	Oo
_____	_____	_____	_____	Tt
Uu	_____	_____	_____	_____

_____

Write the missing letters. Say the letters.

A a	Bb	C_	Dd	__e	Ff	G_
__h	I__	Jj	Kk	__l	M__	Nn
Oo	Pp	Q_	__r	Ss	__t	Uu
__v	W__	Xx	__y	Zz		

 1.1 Imperative Verb Form

Start Talking

Ask a classmate.

A: Hello. My name is _____.

What's your name?

B: My name is _____.

A: Please write your name.

Write your name. Ask two classmates to write their names.

Name: _____.

Name: _____.

Name: _____.

Start Talking

Ask the teacher. Ask a classmate.

A: What's your first name?

B: My first name is _____.

A: Please spell your first name.

B: — .

A: What's your last name?

B: My last name is _____.

A: Please write your last name.

B: — .

Write your name. Write the names of two classmates.

Name: _____   _____
        (First)   (Last)

Name: _____   _____
        (First)   (Last)

Name: _____   _____
        (First)   (Last)

1.2 Possessive Adjectives

Look Again

Write.

Ll _____ _____ _____ _____ .

Rr _____ _____ _____ _____ .

Listen and repeat.

1. **l**ast
2. **l**etter
3. **l**isten
4. he**ll**o
5. spe**ll**
6. **r**ead
7. **r**epeat
8. w**r**ite
9. fi**r**st
10. you**r**

Listen and write **l** or **r**.

1. w_ r _ite
2. __etter
3. c__ass
4. th__ee
5. ci__cle
6. wo__d
7. p__ease
8. schoo__

Listen and write the word.

1. Please say your ____first___ name.

2. Please _____ your name.

3. Please _____ your name.

4. Please _____ for your name.

Look Again

 Look and listen. Do the actions.

Print your name.

Read your name.

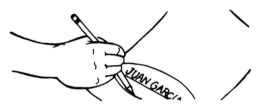

Circle your name.

Sign your name.

Ask a classmate to do the actions. Write the actions.

1. _____

2. _____

3. _____

4. _____

Talk to your classmates.

A: Hello. My name is _____.

B: Hi. I am _____.

A: Nice to meet you.

B: Nice to meet you, too.

A: Hello. My name's _____.

B: Hi. I'm _____.

A: Glad to meet you.

B: Glad to meet you, too.

Introduce classmates.

A: This is _____.

B: Pleased to meet you.

C: Pleased to meet you, too.

Write the country names. Write the nationalities.

Country		**Nationality**
Teacher:	_____	_____
Classmates:	_____	_____
	_____	_____
	_____	_____
	_____	_____

Ask a classmate. Ask the teacher.

A: Where are you from?

B: I'm from _____.

A: What nationality are you?

B: I'm _____.

 ## Listen to the story. Number the pictures.

San Francisco, California

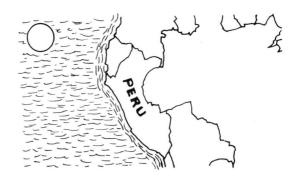

Tell the story. Write the story.

His name _____ Ramon Perez. He is _____ Peru.

_____ is married. His wife's _____ is Teresa. They

have _____ children. _____ live in California.

1.3 Present Tense *to be*

TWO-WAY REVIEW

Work with a partner. One of you works with this page.
The other works with page 23. Don't look at your
partner's page.

Ask your partner.

1. What's your last name?
2. Please spell your first name.
3. Where are you from?
4. Are you American?

Circle the answer.

1. I am American.
   My first name is Ann.

2. My last name is Smith.
   S-M-I-T-H.

3. I'm married.
   I'm American.

4. I have three children.
   Yes, I am.

ON YOUR OWN

Fill out the form. Please print. Tell about yourself.

Last Name,	First Name
Country	
Nationality	
Signature	

TWO-WAY REVIEW

Work with a partner. One of you works with this page. The other works with page 22. Don't look at your partner's page.

Circle the answer.

1. My first name is Susan.
My last name is Lee.

2. S-U-S-A-N.
Nice to meet you.

3. I'm from China.
I'm Chinese.

4. I'm married.
No, I'm not.

Ask your partner.

1. What's your first name?
2. What's your last name?
3. What nationality are you?
4. Are you married?

ON YOUR OWN

Fill out the form. Please print. Tell about yourself.

Last Name,	First Name
Country	
Nationality	
Signature	

Write the alphabet.

_____ A a _____   _____   _____   _____   _____

_____   _____   _____   _____   _____

_____   _____   _____   _____   _____

_____   _____   _____   _____   _____

_____

Circle each word. Copy the questions. Ask a classmate.

1. (What's)(your)(name)?   _What's your name?_ _____

2. What'syourfirstname?   _____

3. What'syourlastname?   _____

4. Whereareyoufrom?   _____

5. What'syournationality?   _____

6. Areyoumarried?   _____

Read the story on page 134. Write about yourself. Answer questions 1–6 above. Read your story in class.

The Calendar

Words

eleven	fifteen	nineteen	fifty	ninety
twelve	sixteen	twenty	sixty	one hundred
thirteen	seventeen	thirty	seventy	
fourteen	eighteen	forty	eighty	

1	2	3	4	5	6	7	8	9	10
11	12	13	14	15	16	17	18	19	20
21	22	23	24	25	26	27	28	29	30
31	32	33	34	35	36	37	38	39	40
41	42	43	44	45	46	47	48	49	50
51	52	53	54	55	56	57	58	59	60
61	62	63	64	65	66	67	68	69	70
71	72	73	74	75	76	77	78	79	80
81	82	83	84	85	86	87	88	89	90
91	92	93	94	95	96	97	98	99	100

 Listen and repeat the numbers.
Say the words.

Listen and write the telephone numbers.

1. 7 3 4 - _2_ 8 6 1

2. 2 1 9 - 0 3 ___ 7

3. 4 ___ 2 - 8 7 9 6

4. 8 6 1 - 6 0 0 ___

5. 9 ___ 7 - 4 3 0 9

6. ___ 3 2 - 0 7 0 4

Listen and circle the number.

1. 5	15	(50)
2. 18	8	89
3. 70	7	17
4. 19	90	9
5. one	five	nine
6. three	thirty	thirteen
7. sixteen	six	sixty
8. four	forty	fourteen

Listen and write the numbers.

1. Repeat number _____*twenty*_____.

2. Write number _____.

3. Spell number _____.

4. What is number _____?

5. Please give me number _____.

Start Talking

Ask a classmate. Ask the teacher.

Telephone = Tel.

Number = No.

A: What's your phone number?

B: _____ .

A: Please repeat that.

B: _____ .

A: Thank you.

B: You're welcome.

Write your name and telephone number. Write more names and telephone numbers. Ask your teacher and classmates.

Name   **Tel. No.**

_____   _____

_____   _____

_____   _____

2.1   Polite Commands

Start Talking

Read the words. Ask a classmate.

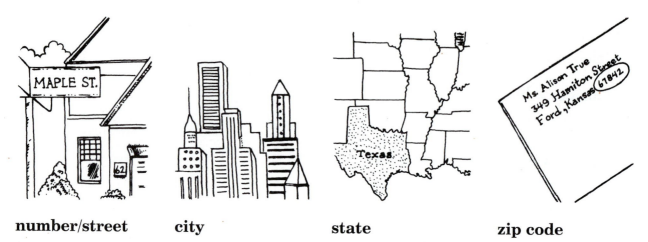

number/street   **city**   **state**   **zip code**

A: Where do you live?

B: I live in _____.
         (City/State)

A: What's your address?

B: _____.
       (Number/Street)

Write your home address. Write your school address.

Home Address: _____
                (Number/Street)

              _____
                (City) (State) (Zip Code)

School Address: _____
                 (Number/Street)

                _____
                 (City) (State) (Zip Code)

 Look and listen. Do the actions.

Stand up.

Take a number.

Sit down.

Listen for your number.

Ask the teacher to do the actions. Ask a classmate to do the actions. Write the actions.

1. _____   3. _____

2. _____   4. _____

Look Again

• • • • • • • • • • • • • • • • • • •

Write.

Dd ____   ____   ____   ____

Tt ____   ____   ____   ____

 Listen and repeat.

1. **t**en   **d**o
2. **t**wo   **d**own
3. **t**wenty   co**d**e
4. mee**t**   a**dd**ress
5. si**t**   stan**d**

Listen and write **d** or **t**.

1. _t_ake   5. __elephone
2. __ate   6. stree__
3. s__ate   7. calen__ar
4. marrie__   8. chil__ren

Listen and write the word.

1. What's your _____ *address* _____?
2. What's your _____ of birth?
3. Please _____ up.
4. Please sit _____.

Read the months and years.

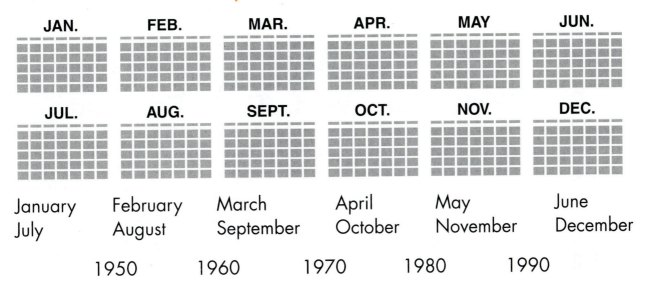

| JAN. | FEB. | MAR. | APR. | MAY | JUN. |
| JUL. | AUG. | SEPT. | OCT. | NOV. | DEC. |

| January | February | March | April | May | June |
| July | August | September | October | November | December |

1950   1960   1970   1980   1990

Ask a classmate or the teacher.

A: What's your date of birth?

B: _____.

A: How old are you?

B: I'm _____ years old.

Write your date of birth.

Date of Birth: _____
                   (Month / Day / Year)

GRAMMAR CHECK ✔

2.2 Contractions with the Verb *to be*

GRAMMAR CHECK ✔

2.3 The Conjunctions *and* and *or*

Read the words.

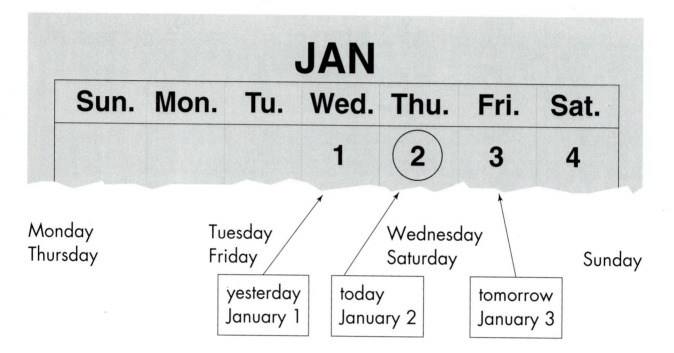

JAN

Sun.	Mon.	Tu.	Wed.	Thu.	Fri.	Sat.
			1	(2)	3	4

Monday
Thursday

Tuesday
Friday

Wednesday
Saturday

Sunday

yesterday
January 1

today
January 2

tomorrow
January 3

Ask a classmate or the teacher.

A: What's the date today?

B: Today is _____.
(month/day/year)

A: What day is today?

B: _____.

Listen and circle the dates.

1. October 21   December 31
2. March 15   May 5
3. July 20   June 30

4. January 13   February 30
5. Tuesday   Thursday
6. Sunday   Monday

Listen to the story. Number the pictures.

○

○

○

○

Tell the story. Write the story.

I live in Boston. In July and _____ the weather is

_____. In October the _____ is cool. In January

and _____ the weather is _____. My favorite

_____ is December. My _____ is in

_____.

2.4   The Prepositions *in* and *from*

Work with a partner. One of you works with this page. The other works with page 35. Don't look at your partner's page.

Ask your partner.

1. What's the date tomorrow?
2. What's your date of birth?
3. What's your phone number?
4. What day is today?

Circle the answer.

1. I live in California.
   I am from Mexico.

2. My zip code is 11215.
   My address is 21 East Street.

3. I am 66 years old.
   I'm fine, thank you.

4. Yesterday was June 4.
   November.

ON YOUR OWN

Write about yourself. Fill out the form. Please Print.

NAME:	_____
ADDRESS:	_____
	_____
PHONE NO.:	_____
DATE OF BIRTH: _____	AGE: _____
COUNTRY: _____	NATIONALITY: _____
SIGNATURE: _____	DATE: _____

Work with a partner. One of you works with this page.
The other works with page 34. Don't look at your
partner's page.

Circle the answer.

1. Tomorrow is March 19.
   Today is March 18.

2. July 13, 1960.
   I'm fine, thank you.

3. My address is 16 West St.
   My phone number is 253-4309.

4. My birthday is tomorrow.
   Wednesday.

Ask your partner.

1. Where do you live?
2. What's your address?
3. How old are you?
4. What's your favorite month?

ON YOUR OWN

Write about yourself. Fill out the form. Please print.

NAME:	_____
ADDRESS:	_____
	_____
PHONE NO.:	_____
DATE OF BIRTH:	_____ AGE: _____
COUNTRY:	_____ NATIONALITY: _____
SIGNATURE:	_____ DATE: _____

Write the numbers.

11 _____	17 _____	50 _____
12 _____	18 _____	60 _____
13 _____	19 _____	70 _____
14 _____	20 _____	80 _____
15 _____	30 _____	90 _____
16 _____	40 _____	100 _____

Circle each word. Copy the questions. Ask a classmate.

1. (Where)(do)(you)(live)?   *Where do you live?* _____
2. What'syouraddress?   _____
3. What'syourphonenumber?   _____
4. What'syourdateofbirth?   _____
5. Howoldareyou?   _____
6. What'syourfavoritemonth?   _____

Write about yourself. Answer questions 1–6 above. Read your story in class.

School

Words

student	pen	book	clock
teacher	chair	notebook	eraser
paper	table	calendar	dictionary

Point to the people and things.
Say the words.

Ask a classmate.

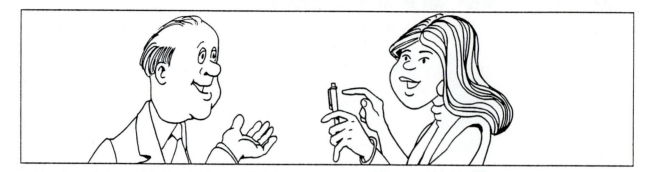

A: Excuse me. What's this?

B: It is a _____.

A: Please speak slowly.

A: Excuse me. What's that?

B: It's a _____.

A: I'm sorry. I don't understand.

Ask a classmate about things in the classroom.

3.1   Demonstrative Pronouns

Start Talking

Ask a classmate.

A: Do you need paper?

B: Yes, I do.

A: Here you are.

B: Thank you very much.

A: What do you need?

B: I need a _____.

A: Here you are.

B: Thank you very much.

Write.

 1. _____

 2. _____

 3. _____

4. _____

 5. _____

Look and listen. Do the actions.

Enter the room.

Turn on the light.

Turn off the light.

Leave the room.

Ask the teacher to do the actions. Ask a classmate to do the actions. Write the actions.

1. _____

2. _____

3. _____

4. _____

Look Again

Write

Ff _____   _____   _____   _____

Vv _____   _____   _____   _____

Listen and repeat.

1. **f**our   **v**erb
2. **f**rom   **v**ery
3. **fi**fty   se**v**en
4. wi**f**e   lea**v**e
5. o**ff**   ha**v**e

Listen and write **f** or **v**.

1. ___or
2. No___ember
3. ___i___teen
4. li___e
5. ___riday
6. twel___e
7. ___i___e
8. ___ebruary

Listen and write the word.

1. Where do you _____?
2. Are you _____ Africa?
3. Today is _____.
4. Thank you _____ much.

Look Again

When is your class? Put an X on the days and times.

	Sun	Mon	Tue	Wed	Thur	Fri	Sat
9:00 — 12:00							
1:00 — 5:00							
5:00 — 9:00							

Ask a classmate.

A: Do you study English?

B: Yes, I do.

A: On what days?

B: _____.

A: What time is your class?

B: From _____ to _____.

A: What's your teacher's name?

B: _____.

3.2 Present Tense Questions and Answers

3.3 Prepositions of Time

Keep Talking

Say the words. Write each word under a picture.

happy   confused   interested   busy   nervous   bored

_____   _____   _____

_____   _____   _____

Ask a classmate.

A: Are you confused?   **A:** Are you nervous?

B: (Yes, I am.)   **B:** (No, I'm not.)

Ask your teacher and classmates. Write *yes* or *no*.

Name	Happy	Busy	Confused	Nervous	Bored

3.4   Short Answers with Present Tense *to be*

Keep Talking

Read the words. Match each word to a picture. Number the pictures.

1.	talking	**5.**	sitting	**9.**	cleaning
2.	reading	**6.**	standing	**10.**	putting
3.	writing	**7.**	teaching	**11.**	giving
4.	listening	**8.**	pointing	**12.**	taking

Ask a classmate.

A: Are you busy?

B: Yes, I am.

A: What are you doing?

B: I'm reading a book.

3.5 Present Continuous Statements

Look at the picture. Listen to the story.

Tell the story. Write the story.

It is _____ morning. I _____ in class. The

_____ is _____. The _____ are

_____. One student is _____. Another student is

confused. We are all _____.

Work with a partner. One of you works with this page. The other works with page 47. Don't look at your partner's page.

Ask your partner.

1. What's this?
2. What are you doing?
3. What time is your class?
4. What's your teacher's name?

Circle the answer.

1. It's an eraser.
   Thank you.

2. I'm fine.
   Yes, I need paper.

3. Yes, I do.
   Yes, I am.

4. From 6:00 to 8:00 P.M.
   From Monday to Friday.

Spell the words to your partner. Write the letters you hear.

1. T H U R S D A Y
2. A U G U S T
3. C A L E N D A R
4. S T U D E N T

1. _ _ _ _ _ _ _ _ _
2. _ _ _ _ _ _ _ _ _
3. _ _ _ _ _ _ _ _ _
4. _ _ _ _ _ _ _ _ _

Work with a partner. One of you works with this page. The other works with page 46. Don't look at your partner's page.

Circle the answer.

1. Three o'clock.
It's a calendar.

2. I'm confused.
I'm writing in my notebook.

3. From 9:00 to 12:00.
Yes, I am.

4. I'm a student.
His name is Mr. Kim.

Ask your partner.

1. What's that?
2. Do you need paper?
3. Do you study English?
4. What time is your class?

Write the letters you hear. Spell the words to your partner.

1. _ _ _ _ _ _ _ _ _

2. _ _ _ _ _ _ _ _ _

3. _ _ _ _ _ _ _ _

4. _ _ _ _ _ _ _ _

1. F R I D A Y

2. J A N U A R Y

3. S C H O O L

4. C L O C K

Find the words.

school	time	teacher	month
class	day	student	year

```
D  T  E  A  C  H  E  R  R  T
O  A  C  L  L  M  T  N  M  Y
D  A  Y  A  A  T  T  I  M  E
C  L  A  S  S  N  T  M  E  A
Y  E  A  S  C  H  O  O  L  R
S  T  U  D  E  N  T  T  N  T
S  T  D  N  M  O  N  T  H  H
```

Circle each word. Copy the questions. Ask a classmate.

1. DoyoustudyEnglish?   _____

2. Whattimeisyourclass?   _____

3. Whatdayisyourclass?   _____

4. What'syourteacher'sname?   _____

5. Whatareyoudoing?   _____

Write about yourself. Answer questions 1–5 above. Read your story in class.

Time

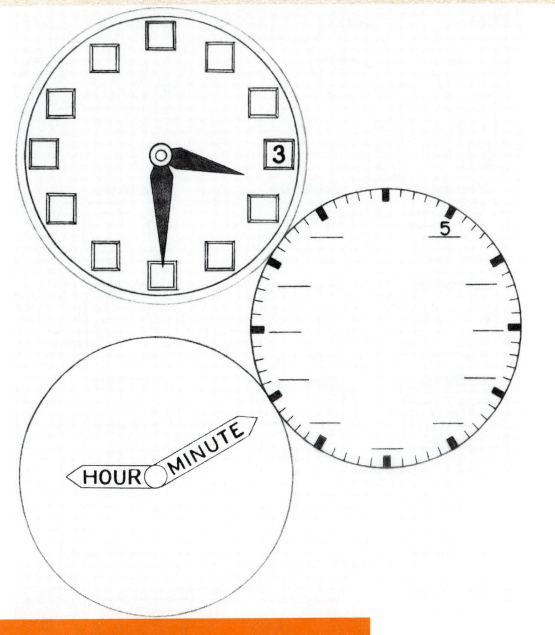

Write the numbers.
Say the words.

49

Listen and circle the time.

1.   **4.**

2.   **5.**

3.   **6.**

 Listen and circle the time.

1.     **4.**

2.     **5.**

3.     **6.**

Write the time in numbers.

1. It's six fifteen. _____   **4.** It's seven twenty. _____

2. It's nine thirty. _____   **5.** It's four o'clock. _____

3. It's two forty-five. _____   **6.** It's ten fifty-five. _____

Start Talking

Read.

one o'clock

ten minutes to one

**ten (minutes) after one
ten (minutes) past one**

a quarter to one

**a quarter after one
a quarter past one**

half past one

Ask a classmate or the teacher.

A: Excuse me. What time is it?

B: It's _____.

A: Excuse me?

B: _____.

4.1 Questions and Answers with *What time . . . ?*

Start Talking

 Look and Listen. Do the actions.

Set the time.

Look at the time.

Tell the time.

Ask for the time.

Ask the teacher to do the actions. Ask a classmate to do the actions. Write the actions.

1. _____

2. _____

3. _____

4. _____

Look Again

Write.

Bb ____   ____   ____   ____

Pp ____   ____   ____   ____

 Listen and repeat.

1.	**b**ook	**p**en	
2.	**b**usy	**p**ut	
3.	ta**b**le	**p**a**p**er	
4.	num**b**er	ha**pp**y	
5.	jo**b**	u**p**	

Listen and write b or p.

1.	____lease	**5.**	u____
2.	____irthday	**6.**	____eople
3.	Octo____er	**7.**	____efore
4.	____ast	**8.**	A____ril

Listen and write the word.

1. What is your telephone _____?

2. What is your date of _____?

3. Do you need _____?

4. Are you _____?

5. Are you_____?

Ask a classmate or the teacher.

BANK HOURS

MON.,TUES., WED., FRI., —	9:00-3:00
THURS.	9:00-6:00
SAT.	9:00-1:00

A: What time is the bank open on (Mondays)?

B: From _____ in the morning to _____ in the afternoon.

A: What time is the bank open on (Saturdays)?

B: From _____ to _____ .

Write the times these places are open.

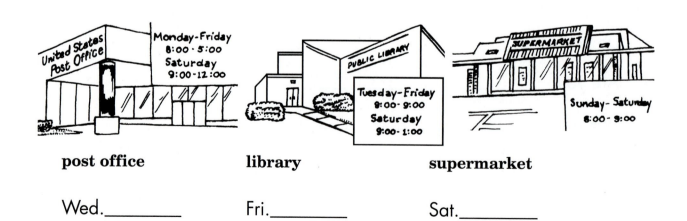

United States Post Office — Monday–Friday 8:00 - 5:00 / Saturday 9:00 - 12:00

PUBLIC LIBRARY — Tuesday–Friday 9:00 - 9:00 / Saturday 9:00 - 1:00

SUPERMARKET — Sunday–Saturday 8:00 - 9:00

post office   **library**   **supermarket**

Wed._____   Fri._____   Sat._____

Keep Talking

Read the words. Number the pictures.

1. start work
2. finish work
3. start class
4. finish class

5. eat breakfast
6. eat lunch
7. eat dinner
8. leave the house

9. come home
10. watch TV
11. go to bed
12. get up

Keep Talking

Ask a classmate or the teacher. Write the time.

1. What time do you get up? _____

2. What time do you eat breakfast? _____

3. What time do you leave for work? _____

4. What time do you start work? _____

5. What time do you eat lunch? _____

6. What time do you start class? _____

7. What time do you come home? _____

8. What time do you eat dinner? _____

9. _____? _____

10. _____? _____

Write about your day. Tell the class about your day. Use the words on page 55.

I get up at _____

_____

_____

4.2 Present Tense Statements

 # Listen to the story. Number the pictures.

Tell the story. Write the story.

From _____ to Friday, I _____ to work. On

Wednesday _____, I go to school. On _____

afternoons, I go to the _____. On Saturday mornings I

_____ my apartment and _____ the laundry. On

Saturday _____, I _____ TV. On Sundays, I

_____.

Work with a partner. One of you works with this page. The other works with page 59. Don't look at your partner's page.

Ask your partner.

1. What time is it?
2. What time is the supermarket open on Saturday?
3. What time does the bank close today?
4. What time do you eat lunch?

Circle the answer.

1. It's March 15.
   It's 3:00.

2. It opens at 8:00.
   Tomorrow is Tuesday.

3. The bank is closed on Sunday.
   The store closes at 4:00.

4. It starts at 5:30.
   From Monday to Wednesday.

Read these times to a partner. Write the times you hear.

1.

2.

3.

4.

1. _____

2. _____

3. _____

4. _____

Work with a partner. One of you works with this page. The other works with page 58. Don't look at your partner's page.

Circle the answer.

1. It's January 13.
It's half past one.

2. It's open from 9:00 to 5:00.
Tomorrow is Tuesday.

3. The bank closes at 3:00.
The library closes at 4:00 on Sunday.

4. At 11:00.
On Wednesday.

Ask your partner.

1. Please tell me the time.
2. What time does the post office open tomorrow?
3. What time does the store close?
4. What time does your class start?

Write the times you hear. Read these times to a partner.

1. _____

2. _____

3. _____

4. _____

1.

2.

3.

4.

Write the story. Use the word *I*.

1. _____

2. _____

3. _____

4. _____

5. _____

Circle each word. Copy the questions. Ask a classmate.

1. Whattimedoyoueatbreakfast? _____

2. Whattimedoyougotoschool? _____

3. Whattimedoyougotowork? _____

4. Whattimedoyoucomehome? _____

Write about your day. Answer questions 1–4 above. Read your story in class.

The Family

Words

mother	husband	daughter	brother
father	wife	son	sister
grandmother	grandchild	aunt	niece
grandfather	cousins	uncle	nephew
male	single		
female	married		

Point to two people.
Say the words.

Write the words for family members.

_____

_____

_____

_____

_____

_____

_____

_____

_____

_____

_____

_____

Role-play. Introduce family members.

A: This is my _____.
B: Nice to meet you.

A: This is my _____.
B: Glad to meet you.

Start Talking

• •

Bring family pictures. Ask a classmate or the teacher.

A: Who's he?

B: He's my _____.

A: What's his name?

B: His name is _____.

A: How old is he?

B: He's _____.

A: Who's she?

B: She's my _____.

A: What's her name?

B: Her name is _____.

A: How old is she?

B: She's _____.

Answer the questions. Make more questions. Ask a classmate or the teacher.

What's your sister's name?
How old is she?

What are your children's names?
How old are they?

_____?

_____?

5.1   Questions and Answers with *How Old . . . ?*

Start Talking

Circle your answers. Write your answers.

Do you have children?   Yes, I do.   No, I don't.

How many children do you have?   _____.

Do you have any brothers?   Yes, I do.   No, I don't.

How many brothers do you have?   _____.

Do you have any sisters?   Yes, I do.   No, I don't.

How many sisters do you have?   _____.

Do you live with your family?   Yes, I do.   No, I don't.

I live with my _____.
I live with friends.
I live alone.

Ask your classmates and teacher. Use the questions above.
Write their answers. Then talk about a classmate.

Name	Brothers	Sisters	Sons	Daughters	Lives with
_____	_____	_____	___	___	_____
_____	_____	_____	___	___	_____

 5.2 More Present Tense Questions and Answers

 5.3 Questions and Answers with *How many . . . ?*

Look Again

 Look and listen. Do the actions.

Open the camera.

Put in the film.

Look through the camera.

Take a picture.

Ask the teacher to do the actions. Ask a classmate to do the actions. Write the actions.

1.  _____

2.  _____

3.  _____

4.  _____

Look Again

Write.

Mm _____ _____ _____ _____

Nn _____ _____ _____ _____

 Listen and repeat.

1. **m**y   **n**ice

2. **M**arch   **n**ine

3. **m**orning   **n**oon

4. roo**m**   so**n**

5. the**m**   the**n**

Circle the word.

1. name   male   **4.** month   not

2. son   from   **5.** mother   number

3. my   nice   **6.** married   single

Listen and write the word.

1. Are you _____?

2. Is this your _____?

3. This is my _____.

4. _____ to meet you.

Keep Talking

Point to the people. Say the words.

| young | big | tall | pretty |
| old | small | short | handsome |

| long hair | curly hair |
| short hair | straight hair |

Ask the teacher. Ask a classmate.

A: Tell me about your mother.

B: She is _____.

   She has _____.

A: Tell me about your father.

B: He is _____.

   He has _____.

5.4 Using Adjectives

Read the words. Write the word under the picture. Ask a classmate.

| happy | sick | worried | funny | angry |
| sad | healthy | busy | homesick | sleepy |

A: Hi. How are you?

B: I'm fine, thank you.

A: How's your (daughter)?

B: She's (sick).

A: I'm sorry.

Circle your answer. Ask a classmate.

Is your mother happy?   Yes, she is.   No, she isn't.
Is your sister sad?   Yes, she is.   No, she isn't.
Is your daughter sick?   Yes, she is.   No, she isn't.
Is your father healthy?   Yes, he is.   No, he isn't.

Listen to the story. Number the pictures.

Aa Bb Cc Dd Ee Ff Gg

Tell the story. Write the story.

My _____ is sleeping in the bedroom. My

_____ is working at the _____. She is very

_____. My _____ is at school. She comes home at

3:00. My _____ is shopping at the supermarket. My

_____ is in the _____ room. She is

_____ a funny show on TV. I am in the _____

eating lunch.

Work with a partner. One of you works with this page. The other works with page 71. Don't look at your partner's page.

Ask your partner.

1. What's your son's name?
2. How old is your grandmother?
3. Do you have children?
4. How's your husband?

Circle the answer.

1. I have three brothers.
   I am a mother.

2. I have two sons.
   My children are two and four years old.

3. She's fine.
   My sister is twelve years old.

4. My husband is Korean.
   She's very tall.

ON YOUR OWN

Fill out the form. Please print.

NAME _____

DATE OF BIRTH _____ AGE _____

(Check) ___ MALE   ___ FEMALE
         ___ MARRIED   ___ SINGLE

NO. OF CHILDREN _____

NAME OF FATHER _____ AGE _____

NAME OF MOTHER _____ AGE _____

SIGNATURE _____ DATE _____

TWO-WAY REVIEW

Work with a partner. One of you works with this page. The other works with page 70. Don't look at your partner's page.

Circle the answer.

1. My children are small.
   His name is Carlos.

2. She is 84 years old.
   He is 66 years old.

3. Yes, I have one child.
   I have three sisters.

4. I am fine, thank you.
   He's very busy.

Ask your partner.

1. How many brothers do you have?
2. How old are your children?
3. How's your sister?
4. Tell me about your wife.

ON YOUR OWN

Fill out the form. Please print.

```
NAME _____

DATE OF BIRTH _____  AGE _____


(Check)        ___ MALE            ___ FEMALE
               ___ MARRIED         ___ SINGLE


NO. OF CHILDREN _____

NAME OF FATHER _____  AGE _____

NAME OF MOTHER _____  AGE _____


SIGNATURE _____  DATE _____
```

Circle the words.

father	married	male
mother	single	female

1. S I G N S I N G L E L E
2. M A R R D M L E M A L E
3. M A R R I E D M R E D D
4. F M E F E M A L E L E M
5. F A H F A T H E R T H R
6. M T H E R M O T H E R R

Circle each word. Copy the questions. Ask a classmate.

1. Areyoumarried? _____

2. Doyouhavechildren? _____

3. What'syourdaughter'sname? _____

4. Howoldisyourson? _____

5. Doyoulivewithyourfamily? _____

6. Howmanysistersdoyouhave _____

Write about your family. Answer questions 1-6 above. Read your story in class.

The Home

Words

bathroom	table	stove	television	rug
bedroom	chairs	sink	lamp	floor
kitchen	dishes	shower	closet	window
living room	refrigerator	toilet	clothes	wall
	cabinet	shelves	bed	door

Point to the pictures.
Say the words.

Listen and look at the picture. Circle *yes* or *no*.

1. yes   no

2. yes   no

3. yes   no

4. yes   no

5. yes   no

6. yes   no

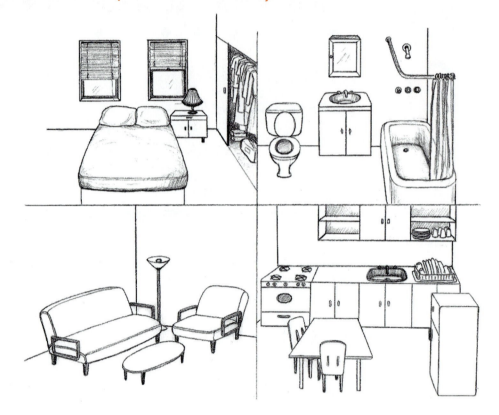

 ## Listen and look at the picture. Write words and sentences. Then talk about your home.

1. There is a _____ in the living room.

2. There is a _____ in the bathroom.

3. There are _____ in the kitchen.

4. There are _____ in the bedroom.

5. _____

6. _____

 6.1   *There Is* and *There Are*

Start Talking

Look at the picture. Say the words.

in   on   under   next to   in front of   in back of

Look at the picture. Ask a classmate.

A: Where's the (soap)?   **A:** Where are the (dishes)?

B: It's (under the sink).   **B:** They're (next to the sink).

Talk about the picture. Write about the picture.

1. The stove is _____.

2. The milk is _____.

3. The table is _____.

4. The window is _____.

 6.2   Questions and Answers with *Where . . . ?*

 6.3   Prepositions of Place

 Look and listen. Do the actions.

   Put the plate on the table.

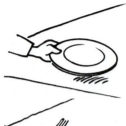   Put the fork on the left side of the plate.

   Put the knife on the right side of the plate.

   Put the spoon next to the knife.

   Put the glass in front of the knife.

   Put the napkin on the plate.

Ask the teacher to do the actions. Ask a classmate to do the actions. Write the actions on separate paper.

Look Again

Write.

Ee _____ _____ _____ _____

Ii _____ _____ _____ _____

 Listen and repeat.

1. b**e**d   k**i**d
2. p**e**n   p**i**n
3. s**e**t   s**i**t
4. g**e**t   g**i**ve
5. **e**nter   ex**i**t

Listen and write **e** or **i.**

1. s___nk   5. m___n
2. ch___ck   6. d___sh
3. n___xt   7. s___x
4. th___s   8. th___n

Listen and write the word.

1. Please _____ a chair.
2. Please _____ the table.
3. There are some plates in the _____.
4. There are some _____ in the cabinet.

Circle the answers. Write the answers.

1. Do you live in a house?   Yes, I do.   No, I don't.

2. What's your house number?   _____

3. Do you live in an apartment?   Yes, I do.   No, I don't.

4. What's your apartment number?   _____

5. Do you like your house?   Yes, I do.   No, I don't.

6. Do you like your apartment?   Yes, I do.   No, I don't.

7. Do you live alone?   Yes, I do.   No, I don't.

8. Do you live with your family?   Yes, I do.   No, I don't.

Small-group work. Ask your group. Mark their answers. Tell the answers to the class.

Name	Lives in a House	Lives in an Apartment	Lives Alone	Lives with Family Members

1. How many students live in houses?   _____

2. How many students live in apartments?   _____

3. How many students live alone?   _____

4. How many students live with family members?   _____

Keep Talking

Read the words. Write each action under a picture.

cook dinner   mop the floor   clean the apartment   pay the bills
do the laundry   wash the dishes   do the shopping   iron the clothes

1. _____

5. _____

2. _____

6. _____

3. _____

7. _____

4. _____

8. _____

Keep Talking

What do you do each day? Ask a classmate or the teacher.

A: When do you (do the shopping)?
B: I (do the shopping) on (Monday afternoon).
A: When do you (clean your apartment)?
B: I (clean my apartment) on Saturday morning.

Write your answers. Ask a classmate.

1. Who cooks in your family? _____

2. Who washes the dishes? _____

3. Who pays the bills? _____

4. Who cleans the house? _____

5. Who does the laundry? _____

6. Who does the shopping? _____

 6.4 Questions and Answers with *Who . . . ?*

 ## Listen to the story. Number the pictures.

Tell the story. Write the story.

Every morning Mariana _____ at 6:00. She

_____ a shower. After that she _____

breakfast. After breakfast she _____ to work and her children

go to school.

Every evening Mariana _____ dinner with her children at

7:00. Then the children _____ their homework. After that, they

all _____ television.

Work with a partner. One of you works with this page. The other works with page 83. Don't look at your partner's page.

Ask your partner.

1. Where's the bathroom?
2. Do you live in an apartment?

Circle the answer.

1. The kitchen is next to the bathroom.
   It's next to the sofa in the living room.

2. My apartment number is 12 D.
   I live on South Street.

Ask your partner. Draw these things on your picture.

1. Where's the soap?
2. Where's the stove?

3. Where are the spoons?
4. Where are the plates?

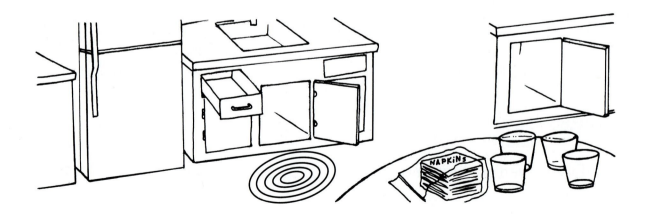

· · · · · · · · · · · · · · · · · · · ·

Work with a partner. One of you works with this page. The other works with page 82. Don't look at your partner's page.

TWO-WAY REVIEW

Circle the answer.

1. It's next to the bedroom.
There are two bedrooms.

2. Yes, I live alone.
No, I live in a house.

Ask your partner.

1. Where's the telephone?
2. What's your apartment number?

Ask your partner. Draw these things on your picture.

1. Where's the rug?
2. Where's the refrigerator?

3. Where are the napkins?
4. Where are the glasses?

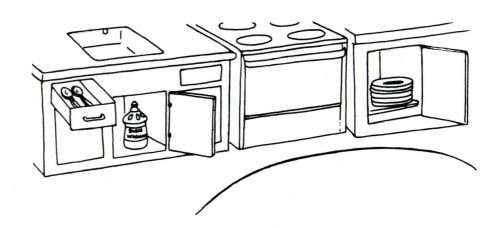

Write nine words from page 73 on the chart. Listen to the teacher. Put an X on each word you hear. Three X's in a row wins.

TIC-TAC-TOE

Read the story on page 81. Write about your day. Use words from page 79. Read your story in class.

Every morning I . . .

Every afternoon I . . .

Every evening I . . .

Food

Words

Fruits		Vegetables			
apples	oranges	broccoli	garlic	peppers	yams
bananas	pears	carrots	lettuce	potatoes	
grapes		eggplant	onions	tomatoes	

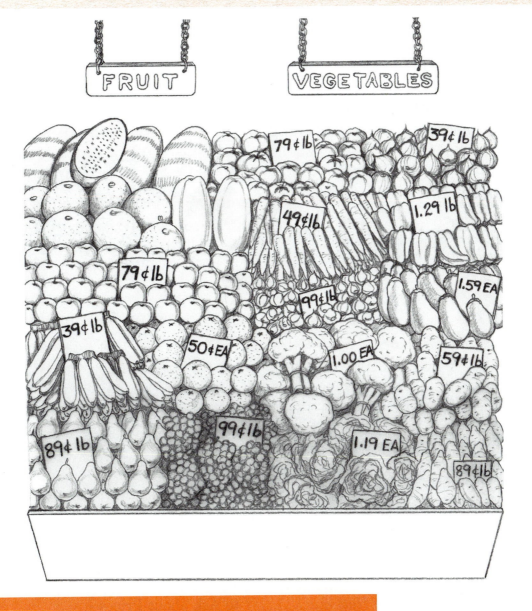

Point to the pictures.
Say the words.

Read the words.

a bag   **a pound**   **each**   **cents**   **a dollar**

 Look and listen. Circle the sentence you hear.

1. Carrots are 39 cents a bag.
Cabbage is 39 cents a pound.

2. The potatoes are 99 cents a bag.
The tomatoes are 99 cents a pound.

3. Peppers are three for $1.00.
Broccoli are $1.00 each.

4. The oranges are 50 cents each.
The grapes are $1.20 a pound.

Look at the picture on page 85.
Listen and write the words and prices. Ask a classmate.

1. How much is the _____ ? _____

2. How much is the _____ ? _____

3. How much are the _____ ? _____

4. How much are the _____ ? _____

 GRAMMAR CHECK   **7.1**   Using *How much . . . ?* to Ask about Prices

Start Talking

Ask your classmates. Ask the teacher.

A: Do you like (apples)?

B: _____

A: Do you like (broccoli)?

B: _____

A: What's your favorite fruit?

B: _____

A: What's your favorite vegetable?

B: _____

Write the answers. Talk about the answers.

	Name	Like/Likes	Don't Like/Doesn't Like
1.			
2.			
3.			

List fruits and vegetables from your home country. Talk about them.

7.2 **More Present Tense Questions and Answers**

Read the words. Match each word to a picture. Number the pictures.

1. eggs	**5.** tea	**9.** milk	**13.** cereal
2. coffee	**6.** soup	**10.** chicken	**14.** salad
3. juice	**7.** sandwich	**11.** fish	**15.** bread
4. beef	**8.** noodles	**12.** beans	**16.** rice

Ask a classmate. Ask the teacher.

A: What do you eat for breakfast?

B: _____

A: What do you eat for lunch?

B: _____

A: What time do you eat lunch?

B: _____

A: What do you eat for dinner?

B: _____

Read. Say the words.

every day

once a week

twice a month

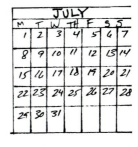

never

Answer the questions. Make more questions. Ask your classmates and teacher.

A: How often do you eat (fruit)?

B: (I eat fruit every day.)

A: How often do you eat _____?

B: I eat _____ once a week.

A: How often do you eat _____?

I eat _____ twice a month.

A: How often do you eat _____?

B: I never eat _____.

7.3   Questions and Answers with *How often . . . ?*

Look Again

Write.

Jj _____ _____ _____ _____

Yy _____ _____ _____ _____

Listen and repeat.

1. **y**ard   **j**ob
2. **y**am   **j**am
3. **y**ear   **j**eans
4. **y**our   **J**une
5. **y**oung   **J**ohn

Listen and circle the word.

1. yam   jam
2. juice   you
3. young   job
4. June   your
5. John   young
6. jet   yes

Listen and write the word.

1. Do you have _____?

2. Do you have orange _____?

3. Is your teacher _____?

4. Is your birthday in _____?

Keep Talking

 Look and listen. Do the actions.

Wash the fruit.

Peel the fruit.

Slice the fruit.

Mix the fruit in a bowl.

Serve the fruit salad.

Ask the teacher to do the actions. Ask a classmate to do the actions. Write the actions.

1. _____

2. _____

3. _____

4. _____

5. _____

Say the words. Write each word under a picture.

chop   soak   bake
boil   fry   broil

1. _____   2. _____   3. _____

4. _____   5. _____   6. _____

Ask a classmate.

A: How do you cook rice?   **A:** How do you cook potatoes?

B: You _____ it.   **B:** You _____ them.

A: How long do you cook rice?   **A:** How long do you cook potatoes?

B: For _____.   **B:** For _____.

 7.4   Questions and Answers with *How . . . ?*

 Listen to the recipe. Number the pictures.

Say the recipe in your own words. Write the recipe.

How to Make an Onion Omelet

1. _____ the eggs.

2. _____ the onions.

3. _____ the onions.

4. _____ the onions to the eggs.

5. _____ the stove.

6. _____ vegetable oil in a pan.

7. _____ the eggs and onions.

8. _____ the omelet with potatoes and a salad.

Work with a partner. One of you works with this page. The other works with page 95. Don't look at your partner's page.

Ask your partner.

1. Do you like tomatoes?
2. What vegetables do you like?
3. What do you like to eat for breakfast?
4. How do you cook rice and beans?

Circle the answer.

1. I like grapes.
   I want to buy apples.

2. I don't like pears.
   They are $.69 a pound.

3. I eat rice, beans, and fish.
   I eat dinner at 7:00 P.M.

4. I eat meat once a week.
   I like to eat pasta.

Ask your partner what vegetables he or she has. Ask how much they are. Make a list.

	Vegetable	Price
1.	_____	_____
2.	_____	_____
3.	_____	_____
4.	_____	_____
5.	_____	_____

$.70/lb.
apples

$.75 each
oranges

$.49/lb.
bananas

$.99/lb.
pears

$1.19/lb.
grapes

Work with a partner. One of you works with this page. The other works with page 94. Don't look at your partner's page.

Circle the answer.

1. No, I don't like potatoes.
Yes, I like tomatoes.

2. I like all vegetables.
I want to buy vegetables.

3. I eat lunch at 12:00.
I like to eat cereal with milk.

4. I boil the rice and beans.
I like to eat rice and beans.

Ask your partner.

1. What fruits do you like?
2. How much are the pears?
3. What do you eat for dinner?
4. How often do you eat meat?

Ask your partner what fruits he or she has. Ask how much they are. Make a list.

Fruit	Price
1. _____	_____
2. _____	_____
3. _____	_____
4. _____	_____
5. _____	_____

broccoli   carrots   lettuce   tomotoes   peppers

$1.00 each $.49/lb. $.39/lb. $.79/lb. $1.49/lb.

Write nine words from page 85 on the chart. Listen to the teacher. Put an X on each word you hear. Three X's in a row wins.

TIC-TAC-TOE

Write a recipe from your home country. Read it or tell the class about it.

Name of recipe: _____

How to make it: _____

_____

_____

_____

Health

Words

head	eye	neck	arm	leg
hair	ear	chest	elbow	knee
face	mouth	stomach	hand	feet
nose	teeth	back	fingers	toes

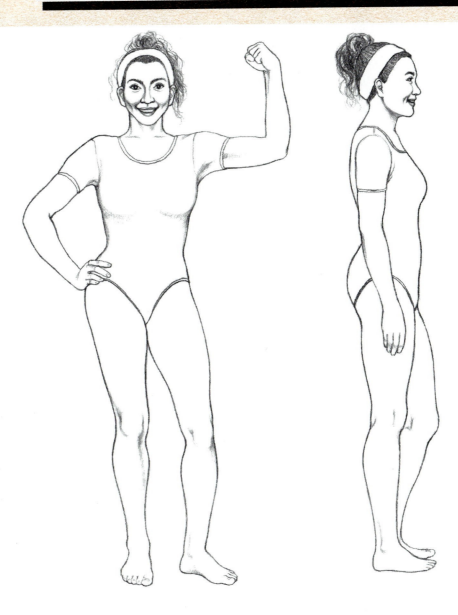

Say the words.
Point to the picture.

Listen and circle the words you hear.

1.	She has long	arms	fingers	legs
2.	She has round	eyes	ears	arms
3.	She has a small	hand	head	nose
4.	She has healthy	hair	eyes	teeth
5.	He has curly	hair	eyes	teeth
6.	He has thin	fingers	arms	legs
7.	He has big	feet	ears	toes
8.	He has a handsome	back	face	mouth

Listen and read the words. Write a number in each blank.

1. elbow	**4.** stomach	**7.** hand	**10.** eyes
2. leg	**5.** shoulder	**8.** foot	
3. head	**6.** knee	**9.** chest	

8.1   Adjectives

Start Talking

Ask a classmate or the teacher.

A: How are you?

B: I'm sick.

A: What's the matter?

B: My head hurts.

Write the sentences. Practice with a partner. Use the conversation above.

1. My _____ hurts.

2. _____

3. _____

4. I have a pain in my _____.

5. _____

6. _____

Start Talking

Read.

cough

cold

fever

headache

sore throat

Ask a classmate.

A: What's the problem?

B: I have (a fever).

A: That's too bad. When did it start?

B: Three days ago.

Answer. Then ask a classmate. Use these words.

SEPTEMBER						
S	M	T	W	Th	F	S
①	②	③	④	⑤	⑥	
⑦	⑧	⑨	⑩	⑪	⑫	⑬
⑭	⑮	⑯	⑰	⑱	⑲	⑳
㉑	㉒	㉓	㉔	㉕	㉖	㉗
㉘	㉙	㉚				

always

SEPTEMBER						
S	M	T	W	Th	F	S
	1	2	③	4	5	6
7	8	⑨	10	11	12	13
14	15	16	17	18	19	⑳
21	22	23	㉔	25	26	27
28	㉙	30				

sometimes

SEPTEMBER						
S	M	T	W	Th	F	S
	1	2	3	4	5	6
7	8	9	10	11	12	13
14	15	16	17	18	19	20
21	22	23	24	25	26	27
28	29	30				

never

1. How often do you have a cough? _____

2. How often do you have a fever? _____

3. How often do you have a cold? _____

4. How often do you have a headache? _____

8.2 Adverbs of Frequency

Look Again

Write.

Ss _____ _____ _____ _____

Zz _____ _____ _____ _____

Listen and repeat.

1. **s**ee   **z**ebra
2. **S**ue   **z**oo
3. **s**ip   **z**ip
4. bu**s**   bu**zz**
5. gla**ss**   ja**zz**

Listen and write **s** or **z.**

1. ___ad   4. ___even
2. ___ip   5. ___ero
3. ___oo   6. ___ee

Listen and write the word.

1. I feel so _____ today.
2. I want to _____ a movie.
3. I want to go to the _____.
4. My _____ code is one-one-two-three-_____.

Look Again

 Look and listen. Do the actions.

Take off your shirt.　　Put this on.　　Raise your right hand.

Open your mouth.　　Take a deep breath.　　Move your fingers.

Ask your teacher to do the actions. Ask your classmates to do the actions. Write the actions.

1. _____

2. _____

3. _____

4. _____

5. _____

6. _____

Read. Role-play in class.

A: Hello. Doctor's office.

B: Hello. I need to see the doctor.

A: What's the problem?

B: _____

A: What's your name?

B: _____

A: Can you come this afternoon at 1:00?

B: No, I can't, but I can come at 4:00.

A: OK. See you at 4:00.

B: Thank you.

8.3 **Questions and Answers with *Can***

Keep Talking

Read. Role-play in class.

A: Hello. This is _____.
I'm sick. I can't come to work today.

B: What's the matter?

A: _____

B: I hope you feel better.

A: Thank you.

Circle *yes* or *no*. Ask a classmate or the teacher.

1. Do you exercise?   yes   no

2. Do you eat well?   yes   no

3. Do you smoke?   yes   no

 Listen to the stories. Number each picture.

_____   _____

_____   _____

_____   _____

_____   _____

_____   _____

_____   _____

_____   _____

_____   _____

Talk about the pictures. Write the stories on the lines.

Work with a partner. One of you works with this page. The other works with page 107. Don't look at your partner's page.

Ask your partner.

1. How do you feel?
2. What's the matter?
3. Can you come this afternoon at 4:00?
4. Do you have a fever?
5. How often do you exercise?
6. How's your father?

Circle the answer.

1. I need a doctor.
   I have a bad cough.

2. No, but I have a fever.
   I can come next week.

3. I never smoke.
   I don't have a headache.

4. Sometimes.
   I'm not sick.

5. No, but I can come at 4:00.
   I can't go to work.

6. I'm fine, thank you.
   She has a problem with her eyes.

Tell your partner to do these actions. Do the actions your partner says. Write the actions.

1. Stand up. _____

2. Open your mouth. _____

3. Say aaaahhhhhh. _____

4. Look to the right. _____

Work with a partner. One of you works with this page. The other works with page 106. Don't look at your partner's page.

Circle the answer.

1. I feel sick today.
   I can't work today.

2. I have a pain in my back.
   I can come tomorrow.

3. I need to see a doctor.
   No, I can't. I have to work.

4. No, but I have a cold.
   My leg hurts.

5. I see a doctor once a year.
   I exercise once a week.

6. My brother is fine.
   My father is OK.

Ask your partner.

1. What's the problem?
2. Do you have a cold?
3. Do you smoke?
4. How often do you have a headache?
5. Can you come on Friday at 2:00?
6. How's your mother?

Do the actions your partner says. Write the actions. Tell your partner to do these actions.

1. _____   Close your eyes.

2. _____   Open your eyes.

3. _____   Look up.

4. _____   Look down.

Fill out the medical form.

Name: _____ Soc. Sec. No.: _____
          (Last)   (First)

Address: _____ Phone No.: _____
           (Number)   (Street)

City: _____ State: _____ Zip Code: _____

Date of Birth: _____ Age: _____
                 (Month/Day/Year)

Please check if you have a problem: _____

_____ **Allergies**   _____ **Chest pain**   _____ **Heart problem**

_____ **Asthma**   _____ **Diabetes**   _____ **Eye problem**

Signature: _____ Date: _____

Write to a child's teacher.

Date _____

Dear _____,
        (Teacher's name)

Please excuse _____.

_____ was absent because _____ had _____.

Sincerely,

_____
(Your name)

Work

Words

bank teller	office clerk	driver	homemaker
secretary	store clerk	mechanic	factory worker
doctor	social worker	cook	house cleaner
nurse	machine operator	plumber	

Say the words.
Point to the pictures.

Listen and circle the job.

#			
1.	doctor	teacher	homemaker
2.	teacher	mechanic	cook
3.	teacher	bank teller	driver
4.	plumber	teacher	mechanic
5.	mechanic	plumber	driver
6.	homemaker	teacher	nurse
7.	nurse	secretary	bank teller
8.	plumber	driver	factory worker

Listen and write the sentence.

1. _____. I work in a school.

2. _____. I work in a restaurant.

3. _____. I work in a factory.

4. _____. I work in a store.

5. _____. I work in an office.

6. _____. I work at home.

Talk about these jobs. Use these words.

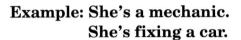

mechanic
fix cars

Example: She's a mechanic.
          She's fixing a car.

office clerk
file letters

seamstress
sew dresses

bank teller
cash a check

nurse
help sick people

secretary
type letters

cook
prepare food

house cleaner
clean houses

driver
drive a taxi

teacher
teach students

Write about two jobs.

_____

_____

9.1   Present Continuous Statements

Ask a classmate.

A: Do you work?

B: _____.

A: What do you do?

B: I'm a _____.

A: How long have you been a _____?

B: For _____.

Write about your job. Write about your classmates' jobs.

Name	Job	How Long
1. _____	_____	_____
2. _____	_____	_____
3. _____	_____	_____
4. _____	_____	_____
5. _____	_____	_____

Talk about your job. Talk about your classmates' jobs.

Look Again

Write.

Ch _____ _____ _____ _____

Sh _____ _____ _____ _____

Listen and repeat.

1. **sh**e   **ch**air

2. **sh**op   **ch**eck

3. **sh**ort   tea**ch**

4. di**sh**   kit**ch**en

5. wa**sh**   wat**ch**

Listen and write ch or sh.

1. _____ort   5. _____est

2. _____elf   6. _____oulder

3. lun_____   7. _____ildren

4. ca_____   8. mu_____

Listen and write the word.

1. Let's go to _____.

2. Let's go _____.

3. Let's _____ the dishes.

4. Let's _____ TV.

Write your work schedule.

	Mon.	Tu.	Wed.	Thur.	Fri.	Sat.	Sun.	Total Hours
Daily Work Hours								

Ask a classmate.

1. Where do you work?
2. What days do you work?
3. What hours do you work?
4. Do you work part-time or full-time?
5. How many hours do you work in a day?
6. How many hours do you work in a week?
7. Do you like your job?

Answer these questions.

1. How many students work full-time? _____

2. How many students work part-time? _____

3. How many students work on Saturdays? _____

4. How many students like their jobs? _____

5. How many students have two jobs? _____

6. How many students need jobs? _____

 Look and listen. Do the actions.

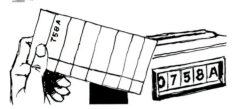

Punch in.

Put on gloves.

Wipe the counter.

Change the sheets.

Vacuum the floor.

Punch out.

Ask the teacher to do the actions. Ask a classmate to do the actions. Add more actions. Write the actions.

1. _____

2. _____

3. _____

4. _____

5. _____

6. _____

Keep Talking

Ask the teacher. Ask a classmate.

A: What was your job before?

B: I was a _____.

A: Where?

B: _____.

A: For how long?

B: _____.

Write about a past job.

Work Experience

Name of Job: _____

Name of Company: _____

Address: _____

Years: From _____   To _____

Talk about past jobs.

_____ was a _____ in _____ for _____.
(Person)   (Job)   (Where)   (How Long)

  9.2 Past Tense of *to be*

Listen to the story. Look at the picture.

Tell the story. Write the story.

Nayda is a _____. She works in a garment

_____ in New York. She is very _____ today

because she _____ a mistake. Her boss is _____.

He says she will lose her _____ if she makes any more

_____.

Listen to the story. Write the story.

Chang is a _____. He works in a _____ in

California. He is very _____ today because he

_____ a lot of glasses. His boss is _____. His boss

says Chang will lose his _____ if he breaks any more

_____.

Work with a partner. One of you works with this page. The other works with page 119. Don't look at your partner's page.

Ask your partner. Listen to the answers.

1. What job do you do?
2. Where do you work?
3. How many hours do you work in a day?
4. Do you work on Sundays?
5. Do you like your job?
6. What work experience do you have?

Write about your job. Answer questions 1-6 above. Add more information. Read your work in class.

_____

_____

_____

_____

_____

_____

_____

_____

_____

Work with a partner. One of you works with this page. The other works with page 118. Don't look at your partner's page.

Answer your partner's questions. Ask you partner these questions. Listen to the answers.

1. What do you do?
2. Do you work full-time?
3. What days do you work?
4. What time do you start work?
5. What time do you finish work?
6. Do you like your job?

Write about your job. Answer questions 1-6 above. Add more information. Read your work in class.

_____

_____

_____

Role-play in class.

A: I want to apply for a job.

B: Do you have work experience?

A: Yes, I do. I was a _____ in _____ for _____.

B: Fill out this application form.

A: OK. Thank you.

Name:	**Soc. Sec. No.:**	
Address:		**Phone No.:**
City:	**State:**	**Zip Code:**
Date of Birth:		**Nationality:**

Work Experience:

Job	*Address*	*Years*

References:

Name	*Address*	*Telephone No.*

Signature: **Date:**

Words

train station	movie theater	park	church
bus stop	museum	bakery	parking lot
hospital	restaurant	stadium	newsstand
drugstore	bar	zoo	store

Say the words.
Point to the pictures.

Listen and look at the map. Circle your answer.

North Street

South Street

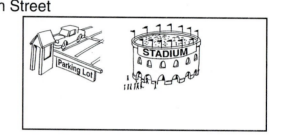

1. Yes, there is.   No, there isn't.   4. Yes, there is.   No, there isn't.

2. Yes, there is.   No, there isn't.   5. Yes, there is.   No, there isn't.

3. Yes, there is.   No, there isn't.   6. Yes, there is.   No, there isn't.

Listen and look at the map. Write the words. Answer the questions.

1. Is there a _____ on South Street? _____.

2. Is there a _____ on South Street? _____.

3. Is there a _____ on North Street? _____.

4. Is there a _____ on North Street? _____.

GRAMMAR CHECK ✓   **10.1**   *There is* and *There are*

Start Talking

Read.

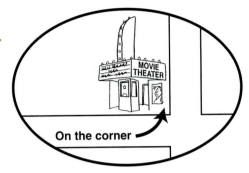

On the corner

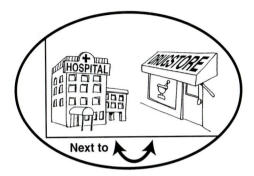

Next to

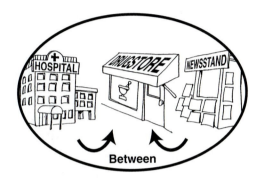

Between

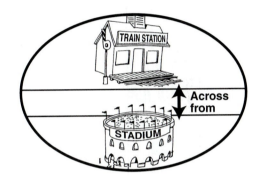

Across from

Look at the map below. Ask a classmate.

A: Excuse me. Is there a (library) in this neighborhood?

B: Yes, there is. It's (across from) the (restaurant).

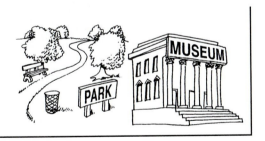

Center Street

10.2 More Prepositions of Place

 Look and listen. Do the actions.

Turn right.

Turn left.

Go north.

Go south.

Walk straight ahead.

Turn around.

Wait for the WALK sign.

Cross the street.

Ask the teacher to do the actions. Ask a classmate to do the actions. Write the actions.

1. _____

2. _____

3. _____

4. _____

5. _____

6. _____

7. _____

8. _____

Look Again

Write.

Th _____ _____ _____ _____

Wh _____ _____ _____ _____

Listen and repeat.

1. **th**at   **wh**at

2. **th**ere   **wh**ere

3. **th**en   **wh**en

4. mo**th**er   **wh**ich

5. fa**th**er   **wh**y

Listen and write **th** or **wh**.

1. ___eel   5. ___ese

2. wea___er   6. ___ite

3. ___ere   7. bro___er

4. heal___   8. ___en

Listen and write the word.

1. _____ is that?

2. _____ are you going?

3. Where's your _____?

4. How's your _____?

Look Again

Ask your teacher. Ask your classmates.

 Do you like to play sports?

 Do you like to watch movies?

 Do you like to read books?

 Do you like to eat out?

 Do you like to take walks?

 Do you like to go to museums?

What do you like to do on weekends?

Look at the pictures. Ask a classmate.

A: Where do you (watch movies)?

B: I (watch movies) in (a theater).

 10.3 Present Tense Questions and Answers with *Where . . . ?*

Keep Talking

Ask your teacher. Ask your classmates.

1. What's your favorite sport?

2. What's your favorite food?

3. What's your favorite color?

4. What's your favorite month?

5. What's your favorite music?

6. What's your favorite TV program?

7. What's your favorite hobby?

Write about your teacher. Write about your classmates.

Name	Likes
_____	_____
_____	_____
_____	_____
_____	_____
_____	_____
_____	_____

Talk about your teacher and classmates.

Keep Talking

Read. Write the dates.

a month ago   _____   two years ago   _____

a year ago   _____   five years ago   _____

Ask a classmate.

A: When did you come to the United States?

B: I came here _____ ago.

Write about your classmates. Talk about your classmates.

Last Name, First Name	**When He/She Came to the United States**
_____	_____
_____	_____
_____	_____
_____	_____
_____	_____
_____	_____

10.4   Past Tense Questions with *When . . . ?*

Listen to the story. Number the pictures.

○    ○

○    ○

Tell the story. Write the story.

Maria Morales _____ from the Dominican Republic. She

_____ here eight years _____. She came with her

_____. He _____ eight years old then. She

_____ a better life for herself and her son.

It was _____ for her. She _____ for a job for

two months. She _____ find one. In her home country, she was a

_____ aide. While she looked for a job, she _____

English. Now she works as a _____ attendant and she

_____ to go to school.

Write your own story. Read it in class.

Work with a partner. One of you works with this page. The other works with page 131. Don't look at your partner's page.

Ask your partner. Answer your partner's questions.

1. What's your name?
2. Where are you from?
3. Where do you live?
4. What's your address?
5. What's your apartment number?
6. What's your telephone number?
7. When's your birthday?
8. Are you married?
9. Do you have children?
10. Do you live with your family?
11. How many brothers do you have?
12. How old is your brother?
13. How many sisters do you have?
14. How old is your sister?
15. What's your mother's name?
16. What's your father's name?
17. When did you come to the United States?
18. What work do you do?
19. Where do you work?
20. What do you like to do on weekends?

ON YOUR OWN

Write your own story. Use the 20 questions above. Look at the story on page 129. Read your story in class.

TWO-WAY REVIEW

Work with a partner. One of you works with this page. The other works with page 130. Don't look at your partner's page.

Answer your partner's questions. Ask your partner these questions.

1. Please spell your name.
2. What's your nationality?
3. What's your date of birth?
4. How old are you?
5. What's the date today?
6. What days do you have class?
7. What time do you start class?
8. How often do you exercise?
9. What's your job?
10. Do you work part-time or full-time?
11. What time do you get up in the morning?
12. What time do you go to bed in the evening?
13. What's your husband's/wife's name?
14. How old is he/she?
15. How's your mother?
16. Please tell me about your father.
17. Do you live in a house?
18. Do you live alone?
19. When do you clean your house?
20. When do you do the laundry?

ON YOUR OWN

Write your own story. Use the 20 questions above. Look at the story on page 129. Read your story in class.

Read.

bake cookies

go shopping

play at the park

go bowling

listen to music

go dancing

visit friends

go fishing

watch a video

go to a party

Ask the teacher. Ask a classmate.

A: How was your weekend?
B: It was (great)!
A: What did you do?
B: I (went shopping). Then (I watched a video).
And how was your weekend?
A: It was OK.
B: What did you do?
A: I (visited friends).

Talk about your weekend. Write about your weekend.

Tapescript

Before Unit 1, Page 3

Listen and circle.

1.	A	**9.**	T
2.	E	**10.**	W
3.	H	**11.**	B
4.	N	**12.**	J
5.	O	**13.**	U
6.	P	**14.**	F
7.	K	**15.**	R
8.	I	**16.**	Y

Before Unit 1, Page 6

Listen and circle.

1.	a	**9.**	c
2.	g	**10.**	r
3.	d	**11.**	z
4.	n	**12.**	x
5.	t	**13.**	b
6.	f	**14.**	i
7.	l	**15.**	e
8.	y	**16.**	u

Before Unit 1, Page 8

Listen and repeat.

0	6
1	7
2	8
3	9
4	10
5	

Before Unit 1, Page 12

Listen and write.

Letters	Numbers
1. r-e-a-d	**1.** 8, 5
2. s-a-y	**2.** 4, 2
3. a-s-k	**3.** 9, 7
4. w-r-i-t-e	**4.** 3, 6
5. l-i-s-t-e-n	**5.** 1, 0

Unit 1, Page 14

Listen and circle the letter.

1.	T	**4.**	d
2.	P	**5.**	q
3.	G		

Unit 1, Page 17

Listen and repeat.

1.	last	**4.**	hello
	read		first
2.	letter	**5.**	spell
	repeat		your
3.	listen		
	write		

Unit 1, Page 17

Listen and write *l* or *r*.

1.	write	**5.**	circle
2.	letter	**6.**	word
3.	class	**7.**	please
4.	three	**8.**	school

Unit 1, Page 17

Listen and write the word.

1. Please say your first name.
2. Please read your name.
3. Please repeat your name.
4. Please listen for your name.

Unit 1, Page 18

Look and listen. Do the actions.

Print your name.
Read your name.
Circle your name.
Sign your name.

Unit 1, Page 21

Listen to the story. Number the pictures.

His name is Ramon Perez. He is from Peru. He is married. His wife's name is Teresa. They have two children. They live in California.

Unit 2, Page 25

Listen and repeat the numbers.

```
 1   2   3   4   5   6   7   8   9   10
11  12  13  14  15  16  17  18  19   20
21  22  23  24  25  26  27  28  29   30
31  32  33  34  35  36  37  38  39   40
41  42  43  44  45  46  47  48  49   50
51  52  53  54  55  56  57  58  59   60
61  62  63  64  65  66  67  68  69   70
71  72  73  74  75  76  77  78  79   80
81  82  83  84  85  86  87  88  89   90
91  92  93  94  95  96  97  98  99  100
```

Unit 2, Page 26

Listen and write the telephone numbers.

1. 734-2861
2. 219-0357
3. 452-8796
4. 861-6003
5. 957-4309
6. 332-0704

Unit 2, Page 26

Listen and circle the number.

1. 50
2. 8
3. 17
4. 90
5. five
6. thirty
7. sixty
8. fourteen

Unit 2, Page 26

Listen and write the numbers.

1. Repeat number twenty.
2. Write number thirty.
3. Spell number seventeen.
4. What is number fifty?
5. Please give me number eighteen.

Unit 2, Page 29

Look and listen. Do the actions.

Stand up.
Take a number.
Sit down.
Listen for your number.

Unit 2, Page 30

Listen and repeat.

1. ten   do
2. two   down
3. twenty   code
4. meet   address
5. sit   stand

Unit 2, Page 30

Listen and write d or t.

1. take
2. date
3. state
4. married
5. telephone
6. street
7. calendar
8. children

Unit 2, Page 30

Listen and write the word.

1. What's your address?
2. What's your date of birth?
3. Please stand up.
4. Please sit down.

Unit 2, Page 32

Listen and circle the dates.

1. December 31
2. March 15
3. July 20
4. January 13
5. Thursday
6. Sunday

Unit 2, Page 33

Listen to the story. Number the pictures.

I live in Boston. In July and August the weather is hot. In October the weather is cool. In January and February the weather is cold. My favorite month is December. My birthday is in December.

Unit 3, Page 41

Listen and repeat.

1. four	verb
2. from	very
3. fifty	seven
4. wife	leave
5. off	have

Unit 3, Page 41

Listen and write *f* or *v*.

1. for	5. Friday
2. November	6. twelve
3. fifteen	7. five
4. live	8. February

Unit 3, Page 41

Listen and write the word.

1. Where do you live?
2. Are you from Africa?
3. Today is Friday.
4. Thank you very much.

Unit 3, Page 45

Look at the picture. Listen to the story.

It is Monday morning. I am in class. The teacher is talking. The students are studying. One student is smiling. Another student is confused. We are all busy.

Unit 4, Page 50

Listen and circle the time.

1. 12:00	4. 6:30
2. 2:45	5. 10:50
3. 8:15	6. 9:25

Unit 4, Page 50

Listen and circle the time.

1. 1:05	2. 2:15

3. 8:14	5. 3:45
4. 11:13	6. 10:00

Unit 4, Page 52

Look and listen. Do the actions.

Set the time.
Look at the time.
Tell the time.
Ask for the time.

Unit 4, Page 53

Listen and repeat.

1. book	pen
2. busy	put
3. table	paper
4. number	happy
5. job	up

Unit 4, Page 53

Listen and write *b* or *p*.

1. please	5. up
2. birthday	6. people
3. October	7. before
4. past	8. April

Unit 4, Page 53

Listen and write the word.

1. What is your telephone number?
2. What is your date of birth?
3. Do you need paper?
4. Are you busy?
5. Are you happy?

Unit 4, Page 57

Listen to the story. Number the pictures.

1. From Monday to Friday, I go to work. 2. On Wednesday evenings, I go to school. 3. On Friday afternoons, I go to the bank. 4. On Saturday mornings, I clean my apartment and do the laundry. 5. On Saturday afternoons, I watch TV. 6. On Sundays, I study.

Unit 5, Page 65

Look and listen. Do the actions.

Open the camera.
Put in the film.
Look through the camera.
Take a picture.

Unit 5, Page 66

Listen and repeat.

1. my	nice
2. March	nine
3. morning	noon
4. room	son
5. them	then

Unit 5, Page 66

Listen and circle the word.

1. name	4. month
2. son	5. mother
3. nice	6. single

Unit 5, Page 66

Listen and write the word.

1. Are you married?
2. Is this your son?
3. This is my mother.
4. Nice to meet you.

Unit 5, Page 69

Listen to the story. Number the pictures.

1. My brother is sleeping in the bedroom. 2. My mother is working at the office. She is very busy. 3. My sister is at school. She comes home at 3:00. 4. My father is shopping at the supermarket. 5. My grandmother is in the living room. She is watching a funny show on TV. 6. I am in the kitchen eating lunch.

Unit 6, Page 74

Listen and look at the picture. Circle *yes* or *no*.

1. Is there a table in the kitchen?
2. Is there a sofa in the living room?
3. Is there a closet in the bedroom?
4. Are there two bedrooms in the apartment?
5. Are there windows in the bathroom?
6. Are there dishes in the kitchen?

Unit 6, Page 74

Listen and look at the picture. Write words and sentences.

1. There is a lamp in the living room.
2. There is a sink in the bathroom.
3. There are dishes in the kitchen.
4. There are closets in the bedroom.
5. There is a table in the bedroom.
6. There are chairs in the kitchen.

Unit 6, Page 76

Look and listen. Do the actions.

Put the plate on the table.
Put the fork on the left side of the plate.
Put the knife on the right side of the plate.
Put the spoon next to the knife.
Put the glass in front of the knife.
Put the napkin on the plate.

Unit 6, Page 77

Listen and repeat.

1. bed	kid
2. pen	pin
3. set	sit
4. get	give
5. enter	exit

Unit 6, Page 77

Listen and write *e* or *i*.

1. sink	3. next
2. check	4. this

5. men   **7.** six
6. dish   **8.** thin

4. your   June
5. young   John

Unit 6, Page 77

Listen and write the word.

1. Please get a chair.
2. Please set the table.
3. There are some plates in the sink.
4. There are some dishes in the cabinet.

Unit 6, Page 81

Listen to the story. Number the pictures.

1. Every morning Mariana gets up at 6:00. 2. She takes a shower. 3. After that she makes breakfast. 4. After breakfast she goes to work and her children go to school.

5. Every evening Mariana eats dinner with her children at 7:00. 6. Then the children do their homework. 7. After that, they all watch television.

Unit 7, Page 86

Look and listen. Circle the sentence you hear.

1. Carrots are 9 cents a bag.
2. The tomatoes are 39 cents a pound.
3. Peppers are three for $1.00.
4. The oranges are 50 cents each.

Unit 7, Page 86

Listen and write the words and prices.

1. How much is the lettuce?
2. How much is the broccoli?
3. How much are the bananas?
4. How much are the grapes?

Unit 7, Page 90

Listen and repeat.

1. yard   job
2. yam   jam
3. year   jeans

Unit 7, Page 90

Listen and circle the word.

1. yam   **4.** your
2. juice   **5.** young
3. job   **6.** jet

Unit 7, Page 90

Listen and write the word.

1. Do you have jeans?
2. Do you have orange juice?
3. Is your teacher young?
4. Is your birthday in June?

Unit 7, Page 91

Look and listen. Do the actions.

1. Wash the fruit.
2. Peel the fruit.
3. Slice the fruit.
4. Mix the fruit in a bowl.
5. Serve the fruit salad.

Unit 7, Page 93

Listen to the recipe. Number the pictures.

1. Beat the eggs.
2. Peel the onions.
3. Slice the onions.
4. Add the onions to the eggs.
5. Turn on the stove.
6. Put vegetable oil in a pan.
7. Fry the eggs and onions.
8. Serve the omelet with potatoes and a salad.

Unit 8, Page 98

Listen and circle the words your hear.

1. She has long fingers.
2. She has round eyes.
3. She has a small nose.

4. She has healthy teeth.
5. He has curly hair.
6. He has thin arms.
7. He has big feet.
8. He has a handsome face.

Unit 8, Page 98

Listen and read the words. Write a number in each blank.

1. elbow
2. leg
3. head
4. stomach
5. shoulder
6. knee
7. hand
8. foot
9. chest
10. eyes

Unit 8, Page 101

Listen and repeat.

1. see   zebra
2. Sue   zoo
3. sip   zip
4. bus   buzz
5. glass   jazz

Unit 8, Page 101

Listen and write *s* or *z*.

1. sad
2. sip
3. zoo
4. seven
5. zero
6. see

Unit 8, Page 101

Listen and write the word.

1. I feel so sad today.
2. I want to see a movie.
3. I want to go to the zoo.
4. My zip code is one-one-two-three-zero.

Unit 8, Page 102

Look and listen. Do the actions.

Take off your shirt.
Put this on.

Raise your right hand.
Open your mouth.
Take a deep breath.
Move your fingers.

Unit 8, Page 105

Listen to the stories. Number each picture.

1. This is Daria. She is sick. She has the flu. She cannot go to work. She needs to stay home and get well.
2. This is Pablo. He fell down. He broke his arm. He needs an operation. He can't go to work. He will stay home and rest for a few weeks.
3. This is John. He had an accident. He is in the hospital. He cannot go to work. He needs to get well.
4. This is Kim. She works in a factory. She had an accident. She cut her hand. She can't go to work for a week.

Unit 9, Page 110

Listen and circle the job.

1. I work in a hospital. I help sick people.
2. I work in a restaurant. I prepare the food.
3. I work in a bank. I give and take money.
4. I work in a school. I teach students.
5. I work for the city. I drive a bus.
6. I work at home. I take care of my family.
7. I work in an office. I work for a boss.
8. I work in a factory. I make cars.

Unit 9, Page 110

Listen and write the sentence.

1. I'm a teacher. I work in a school.
2. I'm a cook. I work in a restaurant.
3. I'm a factory worker. I work in a factory.
4. I'm a store clerk. I work in a store.

5. I'm an office clerk. I work in an office.
6. I'm a homemaker. I work at home.

Unit 9,   Page 113

Listen and repeat.

1. she	chair
2. shop	check
3. short	teach
4. dish	kitchen
5. wash	watch

Unit 9,   Page 113

Listen and write *ch* or *sh*.

1. short	**5.** chest
2. shelf	**6.** shoulder
3. lunch	**7.** children
4. cash	**8.** much

Unit 9,   Page 113

Listen and write the word.

1. Let's go to lunch.
2. Let's go shopping.
3. Let's wash the dishes.
4. Let's watch TV.

Unit 9,   Page 115

Look and listen. Do the actions.

Punch in.
Put on gloves.
Wipe the counter.
Change the sheets.
Vacuum the floor.
Punch out.

Unit 9,   Page 117

Listen to the story. Look at the picture.

Nayda is a seamstress. She works in a garment factory in New York. She is very nervous today because she made a mistake. Her boss is angry. He says she will lose her job if she makes any more mistakes.

Unit 9,   Page 117

Listen to the story. Write the story.

Chang is a dishwasher. He works in a restaurant in California. He is very sad today because he broke a lot of glasses. His boss is angry. His boss says Chang will lose his job if he breaks any more glasses.

Unit 10,   Page 122

Listen and look at the map. Circle your answer.

1. Is there a park on South Street?
2. Is there a church on South Street?
3. Is there a drugstore on South Street?
4. Is there a hospital on North Street?
5. Is there a newsstand on North Street?
6. Is there a parking lot on North Street?

Unit 10,   Page 122

Listen and look at the map. Write the words. Answer the questions.

1. Is there a museum on South Street?
2. Is there a park on South Street?
3. Is there a stadium on North Street?
4. Is there a zoo on North Street?

Unit 10,   Page 124

Look and listen. Do the actions.

Turn right.
Turn left.
Go north.
Go south.
Walk straight ahead.
Turn around.
Wait for the WALK sign.
Cross the street.

Unit 10,   Page 125

Listen and repeat.

1. that	what
2. there	where

3. then   when
4. mother   which
5. father   why

Unit 10, Page 125

Listen and write *th* or *wh*.

1. wheel   5. these
2. weather   6. white
3. there   7. brother
4. health   8. then

Unit 10, Page 125

Listen and write the word.

1. Who is that?
2. Where are you going?
3. Where's your brother?
4. How's your mother?

Unit 10, Page 129

Listen to the story. Number the pictures.

Maria Morales comes from the Dominican Republic. She came here eight years ago. She came with her son. He was eight years old then. She wanted a better life for herself and her son.

It was difficult for her. She looked for a job for two months. She couldn't find one.

In her home country, she was a health aide. While she looked for a job, she studied English. Now she works as a home attendant and she continues to go to school.